RAISING
LLAMAS

TANYA DELLACCIO

PowerKiDS
press.

New York

Published in 2020 by The Rosen Publishing Group, Inc.
29 East 21st Street, New York, NY 10010

First Edition

Editor: Tanya Dellaccio
Book Design: Michael Flynn

Photo Credits: Cover (llama) Mohamed Mohssen/Shutterstock.com; (series barn wood background) PASAKORN RANGSIYANONT/ Shutterstock.com; (series wood frame) robert_s/Shutterstock.com; cover, pp. 1, 3, 23, 24 (llama icon) Airin.dizain/ Shutterstock.com; p. 5 Harry Zimmerman/Shutterstock.com; p. 6 Jerry Voss/Shutterstock.com; p. 7 Alexandra Lande/ Shutterstock.com; p. 9 KeatsPhotos/Shutterstock.com; p. 11 Darryl Brooks/Shutterstock.com; pp. 12, 18, 22 Eric Isselee/ Shutterstock.com; p. 13 Justin Black/Shutterstock.com; p. 15 Sebastian Knight/Shutterstock.com; p. 16 Angela N Perryman/ Shutterstock.com; p. 17 Lisa Stelzel/Shutterstock.com; p. 19 David Gaylor/Shutterstock.com; p. 21 John Moore/ Getty Images News/Getty Images.

Cataloging-in-Publication Data

Names: Dellaccio, Tanya.
Title: Raising llamas / Tanya Dellaccio.
Description: New York : PowerKids Press, 2020. | Series: Unusual farm animals | Includes glossary and index.
Identifiers: ISBN 9781725309029 (pbk.) | ISBN 9781725309043 (library bound) | ISBN 9781725309036 (6 pack)
Subjects: LCSH: Llamas–Juvenile literature.
Classification: LCC QL737.U54 D45 2020 | DDC 636.2'966–dc23

Manufactured in the United States of America

CPSIA Compliance Information: Batch #CWPK20. For Further Information contact Rosen Publishing, New York, New York at 1-800-237-9932.

CONTENTS

LLAMA LIVESTOCK

Have you ever been to a farm? If you have, chances are that there were chickens, cows, and maybe pigs. Did any of those farms have llamas? That's right—llamas can be farm animals, too!

These goofy-looking **mammals** have been around for millions of years. Farmers raise llamas for many different reasons. A llama's wool can be used to makes rugs or clothing. Many farmers raise llamas to carry goods. Some farmers even use them to look after their other livestock animals!

PEOPLE OFTEN THINK THAT LLAMAS ARE ALPACAS BECAUSE THEY LOOK A LOT ALIKE! THE BIGGEST DIFFERENCE IS THEIR SIZE. LLAMAS ARE MUCH LARGER THAN ALPACAS.

HELPING PEOPLE

Llamas are domesticated, which means they're comfortable being raised and handled by humans. People have been raising and using llamas for thousands of years. Native peoples in the Andes Mountains in South America were the first to domesticate llamas and use them for personal gain.

HOW UNUSUAL!

Llamas are strong! They can carry around 75 pounds (34 kg) at one time. They're able to carry that much weight for around 15 miles (24.1 km).

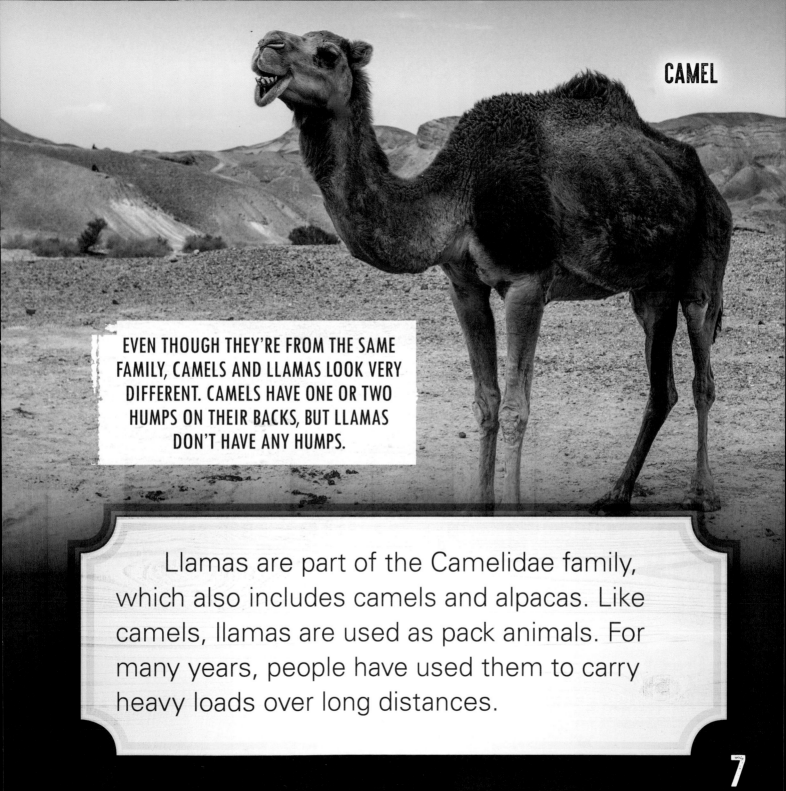

CAMEL

EVEN THOUGH THEY'RE FROM THE SAME FAMILY, CAMELS AND LLAMAS LOOK VERY DIFFERENT. CAMELS HAVE ONE OR TWO HUMPS ON THEIR BACKS, BUT LLAMAS DON'T HAVE ANY HUMPS.

Llamas are part of the Camelidae family, which also includes camels and alpacas. Like camels, llamas are used as pack animals. For many years, people have used them to carry heavy loads over long distances.

SAFE AND SHELTERED

Raising llamas doesn't require many special tools. The most important part about owning llamas is making sure the animals have enough room to **roam** around safely. Llamas are herbivores, which means they only eat plants. They need land with enough grass, other plants, and water to survive.

Llamas also need **shelter** available to keep them out of bad weather. Since their homeland—the Andes Mountains—is dry, llamas prefer to stay under cover when it's raining.

HOW UNUSUAL!

You won't find llamas in the wild. It's believed that this long-necked animal has been domesticated since the 1400s—all the way back to the Inca **Empire**!

HOT, **HUMID** WEATHER CAN HURT LLAMAS. KEEPING YOUR LLAMAS' WOOL TRIMMED AND MAKING SURE THEY HAVE ACCESS TO FRESH WATER WILL HELP THEM STAY HEALTHY.

NOT-SO-LITTLE LLAMAS

Llamas are very strong, in part because of their **stature**. A full-grown llama can weigh from 250 to 400 pounds (113.4 to 181.4 kg). They can stand up to 6 feet (1.8 m) tall from their feet to the tips of their pointy ears!

Because of llamas' size, farmers need to make sure their fences are tall and strong enough to keep their llama herd from escaping. Most llama farmers have fences around 5 feet (1.5 m) high.

FARMERS SOMETIMES USE ELECTRIC FENCES AND WIRE FENCES TO HELP KEEP PREDATORS AWAY FROM THEIR HERD.

FUZZY FLEECE

Most llamas are white, but some are black or brown. Many llamas also have black, brown, or white spots. Their fleece, or wool, has two **layers**. The outermost coat is **coarse**, while the undercoat is soft and wavy.

HOW UNUSUAL!

An important part of raising llamas is clipping their toenails! If not clipped regularly (usually every six weeks, depending on the surroundings), a llama's toenails can curve and force the llama's toes to shift out of place. This can be very painful.

A LLAMA'S FUR CAN BE VERY LONG. IT CAN GROW UP TO ABOUT 10 INCHES (25.4 CM)!

Farmers sheer, or cut, a llama's fur once every one or two years. The coarse outer fur is used for making ropes and rugs, while the finer hairs are used for creating many different things. Llama keepers use special clippers to trim down their llamas' fuzzy wool.

PLANT EATERS

Feeding a llama on a farm is simple. As long as they have enough room to graze, or wander around and eat grass, they don't require much else.

In addition to plants and grass found in the wild, farmers can give their llamas hay for food. One block of hay is enough food to last a full-grown llama one week. After swallowing food, llamas spit it back up and continue chewing on it. This helps them to **digest** it.

LLAMA TEETH CAN SOMETIMES GROW OUT OF CONTROL! PEOPLE RAISING LLAMAS SOMETIMES NEED TO CUT AND FILE THEIR LLAMAS' TEETH TO KEEP THEM HEALTHY.

15

CARRYING CRIA

Many llama farms **breed** llamas, which can make the owners a lot of money. Female llamas give birth to one cria, or baby llama, after carrying it for 11 months.

Baby llamas stay close to their mothers for around six months after birth. After that, the baby llama is old enough to graze the land. Since llamas are herd animals, it's important to make sure the babies stay close to their group.

LLAMAS CAN BE EXPENSIVE. A FEMALE LLAMA CAN COST UPWARD OF $2,000, WHILE A MALE LLAMA COSTS AROUND $500.

LOOKING AFTER LIVESTOCK

Llamas are smart! That's one reason farmers use them to look after other livestock. Choosing the right llama to guard other farm animals is important. The best fit for a llama livestock guardian is a male that's at least 18 months old.

HOW UNUSUAL!

If you ever meet a llama—be careful! These tall animals have been known to spit at people (and other animals) when angry.

LLAMAS WON'T USUALLY ATTACK ANIMALS TRYING TO HARM THEIR HERD, BUT THEY WILL CHASE PREDATORS IN AN ATTEMPT TO SCARE THEM OFF. THEY ALSO MAKE A LOUD, HIGH-PITCHED SCREAM WHEN DANGER IS NEAR.

Though llamas are usually well-behaved with humans, they can be very **aggressive** toward certain predators. Llamas have been known to successfully guard over 2,000 sheep at once!

UNUSUAL HELPERS

Llamas are big animals, but they can be very gentle with the right training! A few places in the United States even allow llamas as therapy animals. Therapy animals are animals that are trained to provide comfort and improve people's lives.

An organization in Portland, Oregon, has five llamas that visit hospitals, schools, and other places to help people feel better! As of 2016, there were 14 llamas that were officially trained as therapy animals.

MAKING SURE A LLAMA IS COMFORTABLE ENOUGH AROUND PEOPLE TO BE A THERAPY ANIMAL TAKES A LOT OF WORK! EACH ANIMAL NEEDS TO BE PROPERLY TRAINED TO PASS TESTS GIVEN BY A SPECIAL TEACHER.

LOVING LLAMAS

Raising llamas may seem unusual, but llama farms have become very popular. There are over 150,000 llamas in the United States and Canada.

Raising these tall and fluffy animals has many benefits. Their wool can be used to make many different kinds of cloth, their strength helps them carry heavy loads for their owners, and their ability to guard other animals makes them useful creatures to own. Llama owners continue to find new and helpful ways to use these gentle animals around the farm and around the community!

aggressive: Acting with forceful energy and determination.

breed: To bring a male and female animal together so they will have babies.

coarse: Rough or wiry.

digest: To break down food inside the body so the body can use it.

empire: A group of countries or areas controlled by one ruler or government.

humid: With much moisture in the air.

layer: One part of something lying over or under another.

mammal: Any warm-blooded animal whose babies drink milk and whose body is covered with hair or fur.

roam: To go from place to place.

shelter: Something that covers a certain place, or to cover a certain place.

stature: A person or animal's natural height.

INDEX

WEBSITES

Due to the changing nature of Internet links, PowerKids Press has developed an online list of websites related to the subject of this book. This site is updated regularly. Please use this link to access the list: www.powerkidslinks.com/ufa/llamas